A Gift for Gifting

B. B. Reed

ISBN: **0692063056**
ISBN 13: **978-0692063057**

Contents

Preface

Introduction.. 2

Chapter

    1. The Anxiety of Gifting.................................... 6

    2. Whom Are You Giving To? 9

           The Experiential................................. 10

           The Sentimental 12

           The New Hotness................................ 15

           The Eternal Kid.................................. 18

           The Perfectionist 22

           The Collector 27

           The Undecided................................... 29

           The Independent................................. 33

    3. Why Are You Giving? 37

           Special Occasions 39

           Spontaneous Occasions...................... 40

           No Occasion....................................... 42

    4. What Are You Giving? 43

    5. Your Personal Touches 46

    6. The Gift of Money 49

Conclusion 56

Preface

When I give gifts, I am filled with joy. It is joy that drives me to inspire you. I hope that through this book, you will discover the positive reactions giving can bring. I believe that our world is off track on how to thoughtfully give to one another. The focus of our gifting lens has shifted to not include people, but to only see stuff. People are what make stuff mean something. Through gifting you need to strive for a deeper connection to those around you.

If you want a more significant link to the people in your life, you need to create more meaningful giving to one another. I have written this book to tell the story of how I give to the people in my life and how, through giving, I have become more in tune with myself. I feel I am able to live more presently and feel connected to those around me in everyday moments.

This book is my gift to you. It has brought me joy to write the story of how I give gifts, and through that story, I hope you will find joy as well. My joy manifests itself in actions that I take to give to the people in my life. My hope is that you will also feel inspired to take action to give thoughtfully to those around you. Through meaningful giving you can change your world.

Introduction

The universe will return in kind what we give of ourselves. With this powerful truth underlying our actions, we have the ability, through the gifts we give, to change our lives and enrich the world we live in.

I am sharing my joy for giving through this book to invigorate you with the belief that expressing yourself through gifting not only benefits those who receive your gifts but can also add meaning to your own life. Meaningful giving will allow you to be more in tune with your emotional self and feel joyful with the awareness of the desires of your friends and family.

The purpose of *A Gift for Gifting* is to provide you with the tools to approach gifting with a new perspective, one based on an understanding of the people in your life and yourself. You will experience giving a gift from a meaningful part of your expressive self.

Gifting is a lost art in our society, and we have also lost the benefits that come with it. I wish for everyone to experience the passion for gifting. A commitment to thoughtful gifting has the power to allow us to capture the human connection that giving to others can provide. You can and should approach gifting in a new way. Gifting is a self-expressive way to change your life and the lives of the people around you.

Most people believe that gifting benefits the recipient alone, but when you give gifts, you emotionally express yourself through the object or experience you are giving. When someone puts thought into a gift, that makes the recipient feel special. The gift becomes larger than its physical dimensions because knowing that someone cared creates such positive feelings. Gifting is a form of emotional expression, and being fully present and open to the joy it can bring to the recipient will bring joy to you as well.

You may sometimes fall into a rut of thinking of gifting occasions as another of life's hassles—one that requires a drain on your resources. But the joyful occasions you celebrate throughout the year do not have to leave you emotionally or financially spent. You experience the best of what life has to offer when you act out of celebration rather than obligation.

Gifting is expressing yourself through something to someone else. There are three parts to every gifting experience. First, and most important, is the recipient of the gift. Second is the form a gift takes, and third is who you are and how you feel about the occasion. You are a part of every gift that you give, and what you put into the gift emotionally is what you will experience for yourself.

Thoughtful gifting will fill your life with rich emotional connections and joy. Expressing yourself freely through gifts will allow you to show off your most positive self. When you design a gifting experience, you create an opportunity to build positive memories of celebrations and human connection. If you pass up this chance to express yourself, you lose an opportunity to participate in the memories that build the future. It's rewarding to capture the joy that is present when you give to others.

My personal joy for gifting has been influenced a great deal by my mom. She always picked out things that made me feel special. Looking back, I see that she never spent the most or bought the best of the best. Her emphasis wasn't on bigger and better, but I always knew how much thought she had put into selecting the things she gave. My mom made gifts—and, more importantly, the act of giving gifts—exciting. The joy that we felt as a family through giving is the foundation of my personal approach to gifting today.

My mom is not only the inspiration for my love of gifting; she is also the reason I took such a deep interest in the experience of giving gifts. Because my mom put so much of herself into giving gifts, through the years we have all tried in return to find the perfect gifts for her. Year after year we would be stumped by the same dilemma: What should we get Mom? So many times my dad and I, in the search for the impossible, would pace up one side of the mall and down the other, trying to find the one thing that would unwrap a childlike excitement.

What I came to understand is that for my mom, the joy and fun in a gift was rarely going to be found in the stores through which we were so tirelessly searching. She was not excited by stuff that lacked an emotional connection. When someone would give her a gift that built joyful memories or reminded her of wonderful past memories, she would light up with excitement. And when someone lights up with joy because a gift has created a positive experience, that memory and connection is felt long past the lifetime of the physical gift.

People are different when it comes to the gifts they truly appreciate. The art of gifting lies in understanding the type of gifts that the people in your life want to receive. With this understanding you can begin to design the perfect gifting experience, customized to the individual people you know and care about.

I know it can be difficult to find the time to search for that special something. With registries and wish lists, it has become easier than ever to purchase gifts without risk or emotional involvement because the items have been handpicked by the recipient. Giving a gift, though, is about building a connection. Items picked off a registry, while safe, have nothing to do with the person giving the gift. A gift from a registry or wish list is often void of the emotional connectedness that should exist between the giver and the person receiving the gift.

You can think back in your own life to when you received a gift from a list or registry. Of course you were happy to receive what you had selected, but you may not have felt closer to the person who gave it to you. Years later, while you may still use the item, you may not even remember who gave it to you. When people receive gifts that simply meet expectations, the experience lacks the emotional force it could have. It is a missed opportunity between two people to celebrate and come closer together. This element of emotional connectedness is vital in creating a joyful and lasting memory.

Gifting has the potential and power to leave an emotional imprint on all of us. Recalling memories from way in the past about favorite birthday gifts or holidays brings back the joy and appreciation you felt for the person who created these emotional connections that you will have forever. The giving of a gift holds within it an enormous amount of emotional wrapping. When you express yourself through the gifts you give, those gifts hold memories the way picture frames hold photos. You retain memories from opening presents when powerful feelings are put into creating a magical experience. Think about the first memory you have of receiving a gift. What made that gift so memorable?

Gifting can allow you to emotionally express yourself and connect with the people in your life on a deeper and more meaningful level. The gifts you give are the physical manifestation of your expressive self and a representation of the joy you feel for the significant occasions and moments in the lives of those closest to you.

If you give gifts out of joy, honor, and celebration, your emotional universe will be full of joy, honor, and celebration. This endeavor triumphs over the things that may try to weigh you down. You have, through gifting, the opportunity to build a network of joyful connections to the people in your life. By being open and expressive with yourself, you are able to be open and expressive with others. Your expressive self can give gifts that are experienced not only in the moment of the celebration but also through impactful memories for years to come.

Chapter 1
The Anxiety of Gifting

Instead of joy, what many people feel when faced with the prospect of having to pick out a gift is dread. That feeling of being overwhelmed by gifting, which is completely natural, ends up leaving everyone unwrapping tension instead of happiness. We place many expectations on the time, money, and effort that are put into the things we give as gifts. The chance that the input will not result in a 100 percent positive output is a greater risk than most people are willing to take. Giving a gift is a gamble, and when it doesn't pay off with appreciation and joy proportional to what was put in, we feel a deep frustration that oftentimes leads to a desire to buy risk-free gifts.

When searching for risk-free gifts, many people end up talking themselves into money, gift cards, or items personally selected by the recipient (from a registry or wish list). There are ways to make all of those gifts personal, but if you choose one of those paths simply to avoid personal involvement, then you close yourself off to the rewards of giving.

Time, money, and emotional expression are commodities that no one wants to waste or expose to vulnerability. Being guarded and careful not to give too much of yourself can feel like a form of emotional protection, but when you act in this manner, you give up the opportunity to have a deeper and more meaningful connection with the people in your life as well as yourself. Bringing joy to those around you through personal gifting enhances your relationships and therefore your own life.

While risk-free gifts selected by the recipients are not wrapped with the potential for uncertain reactions, they are also not wrapped with joy. When you eliminate the risk, you also eliminate the possibility of a gift being amazing and the emotional connections that can arise through positive gifting.

Receiving a gift can be as fraught with anxiety as giving one. Opening something and frantically pretending to love it is not fun! You may feel a great deal of guilt if the gift you receive doesn't represent you as a person or how you want to feel through an experience. Sometimes you are faced with a dilemma of either expressing your dislike honestly (and potentially causing a friend or family member to feel bad) or faking a feeling of positivity (and feeling bad inside). Because the act of giving and receiving gifts presents the possibility of potentially negative emotions, many people wish to eliminate the risk. I feel strongly that even though the desire to eliminate negativity is compelling, it strips your emotional connections and leaves a generic emotional bond, one that isn't special to you or the person you are giving to.

Gifting anxiety can be caused by a lack of confidence in how to make a decision for someone else about something he or she will have or experience. This anxiety can lead to overthinking or second-guessing yourself when shopping for a gift. One year for Christmas, I unwrapped a beautiful turquoise sweater. It was amazing, and I instantly loved it. What happened next? I opened another gift—a second turquoise sweater that was slightly different in style. My husband had purchased the first sweater and then panicked and bought another one from a different store. Although we laugh about this still today, his anxiety at the time was real. He lacked confidence in the gift he'd purchased and felt insecure about when to stop shopping. But he had nothing to worry about: his original purchase was perfect—I wore that sweater even after it had holes in it! To combat your gifting anxiety, you need to be confident in your choices. Tell yourself to stop shopping when you have found what you set out to buy.

In the following chapters, you will discover ways to determine the personality of the person you are giving to and incorporate your reasons for giving in the process. You will also better understand what you are giving, explore the way your gifts will be received, and learn to add personal touches to gifts so they have the emotional connection that makes gifting special to you and the person receiving the gift.

By using the gifting methods outlined in this book, you can combat the anxiety you may feel at any point in the process, whether you are just beginning to design a gifting experience or you are making your purchase. If you understand who you are giving to, you will have a defined path to success in both discovering the right categories to shop from and utilizing the gift recipient's style and personality to give you confidence when you purchase and present your gift.

Chapter 2
Whom Are You Giving To?

A gifting experience should have a balance of the self-expression of the giver and the style and personality of the recipient. As you unwrap the layers of designing a gifting experience, your goal should be to understand the person you are giving to by using his or her personality as your guide. Knowing the personality of the person you are giving to will help you determine how to begin your search. It will also give you the confidence to know when you are ready to make your purchase.

We all have our own preferences as to the type of gifts we enjoy giving. The people in your life have equally unique preferences for the type of gifts they like to receive. As you are aware of how you want to express yourself through the things you give, you must also be aware of the personalities of your friends and family members.

One type of gift will not work for everyone. To truly show your appreciation for the people in your life, you have to individualize the gifting experiences you design according to the person you are giving to. The best way to begin your search for a gift is to identify that person's personality. This will help you organize your thoughts and ideas into categories and details that are specific to the recipient.

If you set out to find a gift without such a foundation, it will be very difficult to choose a gift. The purchasing decision can be the most stressful part of the experience, and I believe that is because you don't know which information to utilize to decide whether something is a good match for a particular person. Organizing your approach before you set out is the best way to build a foundation from which you can make confident and informed decisions. In my experience, people fall into eight general categories reflecting their gift-receiving personalities. Identifying a person's personality can help to guide you in the right direction and pare down the decision-making process so that you can be successful.

By understanding the eight different gift-receiving personalities, you will be able to approach gifting with a greater understanding of how to incorporate another person's unique preferences into a gift.

The Experiential

An experiential person in the context of gifting is someone who values the way a gift furthers his or her life experiences. Life's adventures excite such individuals, and so a gift that allows them to interact with the world in a way they otherwise wouldn't have will evoke a positive response. They are invigorated by the emotions and memories that experiential gifts allow them to have.

People who fit into this category often aren't concerned about "stuff." They would rather plan a weekend trip than purchase a commemorative item to celebrate an anniversary. Traveling, trying new foods, and going to the theater or concerts are all examples of ways that people in this category love to live their lives. Life experiences create lasting memories. People in the experiential category love to dream about adventures big and small, and they enjoy the memories that are created by the gift of adventure.

When you choose a gift for an experiential person, you want to think about what the gift you give will allow the person to do. Someone with this personality wants to go and see something that creates a memory through action. They are typically not as excited by physical objects and are more moved by thought-provoking experiences.

Still, experiential people appreciate personal touches that make an adventure seem specific to them. They like the transformation that experiences allow them to have and the adventure, both physical and emotional, of doing things they love. When shopping for this personality, I gravitate toward tickets, reservations, or gift cards to very specific experiences.

There is an interesting component to gifts in this category: a lapse in time. Oftentimes experiential gifts cannot be enjoyed when the gift is given and received. If you are giving an experiential gift that is not going to take place on the gifting occasion, like tickets to an event in the future, you should also give the person something physical in the moment of the gift presentation that builds anticipation for the future experience. A physical gift is the perfect visual reminder of an experience that is to come, as well as a great keepsake after the adventure.

My husband has been a lifelong Chicago Cubs fan, but he had not been to a game since he was a kid. For our first wedding anniversary, I gave him tickets to a Cubs game at Wrigley Field. When I gave him the tickets, I also gave him a new Cubs baseball hat. The hat was something he could instantly enjoy as an anticipation builder for the game we were going to attend, and it also served as a memento the many hundreds of weekends it was worn thereafter.

Experiential gifts are also great for space-saving needs since the physical accompaniments are often simple token additions. My sister and brother-in-law lived in a very small apartment in Chicago when they were first married. They didn't have room to accumulate stuff. For Christmas that year, my mom gave them gift certificates to a bunch of different restaurants around the city. She wanted to give them something they could enjoy without bombarding them with things they didn't have room for. They loved the experience of planning dates to all the different restaurants and getting to experience the amazing culinary world of Chicago. This gift created a wonderful memory for my sister and brother-in-law and a strong connection for my mom, who knew she had brought so much joy with the gift.

Sometimes two people act as both partial gifter and giftee and plan an experiential gift jointly. For example, a couple might plan a vacation away together as a gift to each person. If you are planning such an experience, you want to make sure to leave a part of the planning to yourself, keeping certain components a surprise. Adding your own personal touches to elements of the experience or token items that will enhance the experience is a great way to add your emotional expression to an otherwise joint effort.

My husband and I planned a romantic trip away for a long weekend one time. We enjoyed planning the vacation together and building anticipation for the adventures we would have, but each of us also planned special things for us to experience together that were a surprise. My husband researched and found an amazing restaurant for us to go to dinner and gave me a dress to wear that fit the occasion (since I didn't know to pack something for a fancy restaurant). I made reservations at a spa for us to enjoy some much-needed relaxation and surprised my husband with some pampering that he would never have thought to plan for himself. This combination of both joint gifting and surprise gifting created an overall experiential gift that gave us incredible and lasting memories.

It's fun to let your imagination take you beyond the confines of what can be shipped from an online store. Experiential gifts are often unique and can create lasting memories. People who daydream about life's adventures can see them come to fruition through experiential gifts.

The Sentimental

Sentimental people are those who value gifts that remind them of life experiences they had in the past. Such people love to think about the gift in the past tense, even while they are opening it. They cherish the old memories brought back by the gift and anticipate the new memories the gift will create. They love when a gift takes them back to a favorite time in their life because it furthers their emotional connection between the past and the present. A sentimental person usually loves to know the story behind why a gift was chosen and how it was found. This helps to create a richer emotional connection between his or her favorite memories and you, the gifter, in the present and the future.

A sentimental person is often most overjoyed by things found off the beaten path. Like someone who is experiential, someone who is sentimental will appreciate extra customization to a gift. These individuals love the idea of a gift being something truly unique and special. They aren't concerned with whether anyone else would think the gift was amazing; they are fulfilled when they feel a gift has personal meaning.

Purchasing something that is one of a kind can come into play with this personality, as such gifts have the potential to be very personal. Finding something unique or unusual that has a specific meaning and significance is a great way to bring joy to someone with a sentimental personality.

One of my favorite Christmas memories from when I was a kid is the time my dad gave my mom a vintage Ozzie Smith St. Louis Cardinals baseball card. My mom is a huge Cardinals fan, and her favorite baseball player of all time is Ozzie Smith. She was speechless and had tears in her eyes as she stared at her instant treasure. I had rarely seen my mom so expressive about anything my dad had given her. It was not an expensive item, but it carried with it priceless wonderful memories.

Finding a gift for a sentimental person in your life can require you to plan ahead. Sometimes the personal touches that make gifts sentimental require extra steps that can't be completed at the last minute.

If you have the privilege of finding a gift for someone who is sentimental, you can use that opportunity to get sentimental yourself! When my daughter was born, my dad wanted to take a picture of him holding her inside his baseball glove. He had taken a picture of me when I was born in his baseball glove and loved replicating the image. So for Father's Day that year, I took the old picture (my dad holding me in his baseball glove) and framed it alongside the new picture (my dad holding his granddaughter in his baseball glove). Creating that gift felt wonderful, and my dad absolutely loved it. It was a gift that truly brought us closer emotionally because it showed such an amazing connection between past and present.

For people with this personality, I like to use the concept "create something that only you could create." The relationship you have with the person you are giving to should be your foundation and starting point when designing a sentimental gifting experience. You should utilize information or access that only you might have to this particular family member or friend. The gift should show this person how special he or she is to you and create connections between memories of the past and present-day moments.

I have known one of my best friends since we were five. Because we have known each other for so long, we have connections that are deeply rooted in experiences from long ago. This gives me amazing opportunities to give sentimental gifts that remind her of our childhood together and further connect us in the future. We used to spend many hours watching *Saved by the Bell* and pretending we were the crazy teenagers from the sitcom. One year for Christmas, I tracked down *Saved by the Bell: Wedding in Las Vegas*, a special episode we had joked about for a long time. What fun I had giving that gift! She loved it, and we had a wonderful time reminiscing about what a funny show we had been addicted to.

When my sister was having her first baby, I wanted to get her a baby gift that was unlike any other she would be receiving. I searched for our favorite childhood books, those I had distinct memories of our sitting and hearing together. A few of the books were not mainstream and thus out of print, but finding them made us both relive the memories of hearing those stories as kids. The gift also gave us an exciting connection to the new little generation that would get to hear the same beloved books that we had.

For Valentine's Day one year, my husband taped paper hearts all over our house, starting with my bedside table and leading all the way down our hall, down the stairs, and around the first floor. On each heart he wrote something he loved about me. The hearts were filled with quirky personality traits that made me feel loved and cherished. This gift was as expensive as a stack of pink paper, but it is still to this day one of the best gifts he has ever given me.

There are ways in every category of gifting to achieve success at varying price points, but the sentimental personality offers the most budget-friendly variety. Because homemade gifts can have a wonderful sentimental component, you can be thoughtful and creative without spending a large amount of money. If you decide to head down the artsy path to achieve gifting success, make sure you put a lot of thought into the person you are making the gift for. The gift should represent and reflect the person's style and personality, so be sure your homemade touches don't overshadow the gift itself.

Making or buying a gift for someone who is sentimental is a gift to both the person receiving the items as well as to you, the gifter. Unlike other types of gifts, sentimental gifts will bring wonderful nostalgic feelings. These gifts make a connection between the past and present, and that leaves a bond that is experienced beyond the presentation of your gift. If you have people in your life who enjoy receiving sentimental gifts, celebrate! Their gift will be a gift for you as well.

The New Hotness

The new hotness person is someone who wants the latest and greatest new item on the market. These individuals are excited by the brand-new versions or just-released items on the shelves. They love the exclusivity that comes with items that have just become available or are in limited supply. Even if they already have a similar item at home: if a brand-new, better model is available, they will be excited about it. They like features and specs and the details surrounding what makes the new item better.

We can all have a little of this personality in us sometimes. It is easy to get swept up in wanting something because it is all the rage, hard to find, or in rare supply. But the new hotness personality takes that desire to a different level. This particular person feels most joyful when a gift is something that he or she didn't even know was available.

Oftentimes my ideas in this category tend toward gadgets and new electronics, but gifts for people with this personality do not have to come with a power cord or an instruction manual. A gift for this person can be a sweater from a designer's fall collection when it is still summer or a spring purse that has just arrived at the store when there is snow still on the ground. That being said, the new hotness tends to not be a money-saving personality. It is hard to find a good deal on something that everyone wants and is flying off the shelves. Planning ahead with a budget or saving up to buy something really special is a good way to make sure you don't get overwhelmed by the price tag these items often carry.

What can be really fun about finding a gift for people in this category is that you can look outside the market they live in to potentially surprise them with new discoveries. Geography can play an interesting role in finding something that is a hot new trend somewhere else.

If you are designing a gifting experience for someone with the new hotness personality, try to identify a broad category you know the person enjoys, and then do a little research to find out what the hot trends are in other geographical areas. If you know that your friend or family member loves coffee, you could put together coffees from local sources as well as new coffees that are popular in other cities. This would allow the coffee lovers in your life to have the latest and greatest not only from the area where they live but also somewhere else.

If you have a wine lover who longs to be on the cutting edge of the latest vintages from the Napa Valley region but doesn't live close enough to really enjoy the exclusive offerings, you could give that person a subscription to a wine club; that way, he or she could receive new wines each month from wineries that might otherwise be out of reach.

People in this category want to know what makes an item special and why it is the best (though not necessarily the most expensive). That means that your gift should include a way for the person to learn this extra information. This could be as simple as telling the recipient about why this new item is so great after he or she opens it or including a note along with a card if you are perhaps not able to share the information in person when the gift is given.

Here is an example of how I might include extra information about a gift I am giving. I saw this scarf among the hot new accessories in my latest copy of Vogue. It made me think of you, and I just knew you had to have it! It will look really great with your green dress. Happy Birthday!

If the gift you purchase is outside the realm of your own expertise and talking about the details would mean staying up late memorizing note cards of information, you can simply include printouts of information (found online or in a magazine) along with the gift.

My husband is one of those coffee lovers I mentioned earlier. He loves the science of making various coffee drinks and experiencing the full range of flavors. One year I bought him an espresso maker. Because I knew absolutely nothing about espresso makers, I found a reliable online source and researched various models, reading reviews and customer feedback. I wanted to make sure that the one I bought had the specifications that would be important to him. After making my decision and purchasing the gift, I printed out a detailed review that I had used as a tool in making my decision. I highlighted key features and specifications that had been big factors in my decision so he could enjoy the information on the new gadget. This extra information instantly made him feel comforted that he had the perfect espresso maker for him.

Even though I am not someone who would typically research a purchase for months prior to making a decision, I know that that is how my husband makes purchases, so it was important to me to make sure that I made my selection for him with the same mind-set. This helped me surprise him with the perfect gift and brought me closer to him. He loved his espresso maker so much that he started making both of us delicious lattes every morning. Everyone enjoyed the gift!

It can be easy to feel overwhelmed when you are shopping for people with the new hotness personality because the most-desired gifts are often too expensive for modest budgets. But if you plan ahead and put thought into a broad category, gift options will present themselves at all levels. Someone with this personality is excited about the cutting-edge, hot-on-the-market aspect of items, and you can find these types of gifts at all price points. No matter what your budget is, you can be creative and design a gifting experience that your friends and family will love. Whether you spend $600 on the latest iPhone or $20 on songs from a great new artist you discover on iTunes, you can find cutting-edge ideas for any budget.

The Eternal Kid

The Eternal Kid loves to tinker and play with new things. This category describes anyone who enjoys gifts that bring out playful instincts. Eternal kids can't help but feel excitement for gifts they receive that invite tinkering.

People with this personality are going to be most excited about gifts that get them involved. Fight the urge to be practical when you're shopping for the eternal kid: you want to think of things that inspire play, no matter the age. Being engaged and involved in assembly or setup is exciting to people who love to tinker.

Again, starting with a broad category is a good way to approach this type of gifting. Knowing how much my (eternal kid) husband enjoys coffee, over the years I have given him unique devices for making coffee and espresso. These were gifts that he could not wait to try out, using the same energy he had as a kid conquering a new video game or building a Lego pirate ship.

If you know or love someone who is an eternal kid, you definitely need to leave your practical adult mind behind when designing a gifting experience. The best way to approach this endeavor is to have fun! Eternal kids don't want what they need; they want something to enjoy and play with. There is a little of the eternal kid in everyone; sometimes it just takes the perfect gift to bring out those joyful feelings. If you are too consumed with practicality, you won't be able to successfully excite the "kid" in your life.

I use the words *play* and *tinker* for this category to remind you of the earliest gifts you received, when stimulating your mind and helping to develop your brain and coordination were the main focus. Even though this book is looking at adult gifting, it helps to remember the joy and excitement you felt as a child when you received things you could instantly play with. This personality still feels that excitement even though their days at Toys "R" Us are past. *Play* doesn't have to mean toys in the traditional sense. Things that are engaging and stimulating to our minds are exciting and help to continue our exploration of the world.

For a significant birthday for my dad, my mom was in search of a special gift. At his favorite woodworking store, she found some rare chestnut wood that was over 150 years old. She decided it was the perfect gift. My dad loves woodworking and was blown away by the unique aspect of the experience my mom had designed for him. What was so engaging about this gift was that there wasn't a specific project to create. My dad was like a kid again! The gift stimulated his mind as he imagined all the things it could become. He couldn't stop touching, smelling, and looking at all the aspects of the pieces of wood and telling us all what made each piece so special. This gift ignited the child in him and gave him an imaginative, playful experience.

Sometimes I think that as an adult you have to give yourself permission to have fun—to catch a snowflake on your tongue or jump into a pool without a care. The eternal kid personality reminds me to smile, laugh, and enjoy the gifts I give and receive. My husband fits into this category in many ways, and when I am designing a gifting experience for him, I often hold the gift or gifts in my hands, move them in different directions, look at them from different angles, and explore how the item or items will be seen when first opened. This exploration helps to remind me to think about his interaction with the gift and to always consider ways the gifting experience can include play.

My mom gave my sister a new workbag one year. When my sister opened the bag, she loved it—it was a beautiful red bag and a great gift. What was particularly fun was that as my sister began to open and explore the bag, she discovered that my mom had filled it with other gifts. She opened every pocket and nook to discover more gifts hiding in all the great spaces. This gift was engaging, fun, and memorable.

Sensory exploration is particularly important when imagining how a person in this category will enjoy his or her gift. Because these individuals want to play with their gifts as soon as they receive them, make sure you design an experience that allows for sensory involvement and instant play. Think about how the other person will see, hear, smell, touch, or taste the gift. For people in this category, the more sensory engagement you offer, the more stimulation they will feel and enjoy.

One of the most playful baby shower gifts I have seen was a laundry hamper. Wow, is that ever important when you have a baby! But this was not just a laundry hamper: inside was a clothesline, and as the mother-to-be pulled it out of the hamper, she found baby clothes hanging from clothespins. This gift was instant fun! Each little gift was displayed and could instantly be touched, seen, and engaged with.

Electronic gadgets are a particularly common adult "toy." Because electronics have to be configured, tweaked, and charged, they are instantly at the top of my list when I think about gifts for people with this personality. But while electronics make great gifts, many times the eternal kid already has every device imaginable, and there isn't anything left to turn on.

My examples in this category do not focus on electronics in order to encourage you to imagine other areas when considering gifts for this personality. You don't want to close yourself off to a broader pool of ideas. I like to begin a gifting search within this category by thinking through a person's routine. I think about what that person does throughout the day, both simple tasks as well as significant ones. Through this thought process, I arrived at a gift for my husband of a really cool interactive alarm clock one year. The clock could be programmed to feed him specifically designed information at particular times, and it gave him more to do than just look at the time. It was an engaging item that I thought of when I imagined his day from start to finish. He is a person who wants to have information from the second his eyes open until the moment before they close at night. Through this idea I was able to find a gift that celebrated something fun about his routine day.

My husband also enjoys the game of golf, but he tends to hook the ball left and lost more often than not. He goes through more golf balls than anyone I know. One year in a fun attempt to give him plenty of balls for a few good rounds of eighteen, I filled his stocking to the top with loose golf balls. It was hilarious to watch him ever so carefully take down his stocking and transfer the balls into a more suitable container. We had a great laugh celebrating his need for more golf balls in a way that made him smile.

Try to look beyond the basic question of practical versus impractical when considering gifts for this personality. This category offers an opportunity to have fun. Even when you give something that is very useful, you can still enjoy designing an experience that lights up the person you are giving to with childlike excitement.

The Perfectionist

When it comes to receiving gifts, perfectionists are people who know exactly what they want at all times and have no problems whatsoever making decisions about what to surround themselves with. They generally do not graciously accept things into their world that do not fit or match the aesthetic they have created.

This category is usually a piece of cake. If you could get inside the person's head for two seconds, you would know exactly what the perfect gift would be. But since that isn't possible, you have to do the next best thing: pay attention to details that are important to perfectionists when they select items for themselves. Putting yourself in the other person's shoes in this category will really help you to remind yourself to not look at choices from your eyes, but to try to see them from the other's perspective.

Because people with this personality tend to know they are super picky, they also tend to be people who have no problem pointing out or saying exactly what they want. They want to control the surprises in their lives by spelling out the things they love. But this can often leave the gifter feeling as though he or she didn't really select the gift. Thus you have to find a balance, designing a gifting experience to the person's taste without succumbing to the ease of simply having him or her select the items.

I was designing a gifting experience for a friend of mine who falls into this category, and I was faced with a dilemma: I didn't want to purchase directly from her registry, but I still wanted to give her something that she and her new husband would love and enjoy for their wedding. What did I do? I used their registry as my guide to understand exactly what things they wanted to start their new life. By looking at specific items they had picked out, I was able to find something that coordinated perfectly with things they were already going to receive from other guests. This provided me the ability to connect and give something personal without forfeiting their very particular taste and style.

My approach to gifting for someone in this category is to select items that have connections to things I know the person likes. I try to remember the details of things I have seen them enjoy and then look for details that match or coordinate in new items.

Paying attention long before a gift is needed can really pay off when dealing with a perfectionist. If a person in your life has this personality, your attentiveness will always be rewarded when gifting occasions come up. If the person in your life talks about something he or she likes or wants, make a note to yourself and hold on to those ideas until you need them. Because people with this personality tend to be open about what is important to them, listening can be your best tool.

Confidence is also extremely important when selecting gifts for people in this category. You can't be intimidated by the fact that the person seems to always know what he or she wants. That isn't a bad thing (says a classic perfectionist), as you can use that information to your advantage. People in this category love registries and wish lists, and while my preference is against giving gifts from a registry or directly off a list, these can be helpful tools in directing you to the right decision simply by allowing you to coordinate gifts to things they like.

Perfectionists like things that go together. Part of the reason they can so easily make a decision about what they like is their ability to categorize things quickly and break them down aesthetically with details that they either relate to or don't. For people who know how to analyze their surroundings, looking at new items is easy—they either match or they don't.

Whether clothes, electronics, or home decor, all things have a style. A perfectionist is always looking for things that relate to one another. Go beyond the basic details of the things people in this category may have or like, and take a closer look at the style and function of what they surround themselves with.

Details are important with this category probably more so than with any other personality. A perfectionist is passionate about decision making. When designing a gifting experience for someone who is a perfectionist, having passion for the gift you give will create the compelling experience this personality really appreciates.

Passion is not a casual feeling of positivity; it's an engaging emotion of desire. Don't just like the experience you are creating—love it! Feel yourself get excited about every aspect of what you select, and get caught up in the details that will be very appreciated by someone who loves details!

I found out that my brother-in-law wanted a new hat featuring his beloved alma mater. He is definitely a perfectionist when it comes to his beloved sportswear. I knew I was up to the challenge, but I would have to pay close attention to the details. I looked at the changes in the team's logo over the years, I looked at the slightly varied options for color, and I made sure I took care to pay close attention to the fit. When I wanted a second opinion about any of the details, I took the time to call my sister, consult my husband, and think through what would be important to my brother-in-law. It may sound as though I spent a week to buy a baseball hat, but in reality I probably spent one dedicated hour. What made the process move so quickly was the time I dedicated to thinking about the person I was gifting and the close attention I paid to the details of the gift. Because of the time I devoted to the details of the gift, it was very appreciated by my brother-in-law.

Gifting intimidation does not help conjure gifting success, and perfectionists can definitely create nerves for the person attempting to excite them. My husband knows all too well the anxious feelings of trying to select something for me when I am not there to point and click. However, with all personalities, understanding how a person selects things for himself or herself will make it clear how to select things when that person isn't present.

For a perfectionist, it's all in the details. Think of gifts for this category as a web. Look at the things the person already has, and think about building upon those possessions with accessories or upgraded features. If a friend of mine had a favorite coat that she always wore, I might pick out a scarf that was a perfect match. Knowing that she loves and wears the coat all the time would give me confidence that a coordinating scarf would also be loved and enjoyed. You could give someone a matching wallet to a purse that she has or a belt to coordinate with his favorite shoes. Building on items that are already loved can be a very helpful strategy when you begin the design of your gifting experience for the perfectionist.

If someone in your life falls into this category and it is someone you give gifts to on a regular basis, you can also think about giving gifts that have additional gifting potential. One year for Christmas, my husband gave me a charm bracelet with just one signature charm to start. I loved the bracelet! He then added charms as the years (and gifting occasions) continued. Because the original gift was so successful, he now has a good foundation from which to work each time he chooses to give me another charm. The original gift helps to guide subsequent gifts in the future.

When you are designing a gifting experience for someone in this category and there isn't a spark for additional accessories, upgrades, or add-ons to existing items or categories, you must forge your own path. If you are giving a gift to someone with a perfectionist personality and the gift is not connected in style, overall aesthetic, or function to things in his or her existing world, you want to think about creating a gifting experience that is complete in itself. Sometimes you have to give a gift along with the necessary supporting accessories to ensure the gift comes already complete. One year my husband gave me a pair of shoes. They were beautiful, but they didn't go with any outfit that I owned, and I rarely wore them. It's not that the item itself wasn't great, but with my perfectionist personality I found it hard to incorporate them into my wardrobe without knowing what to wear them with.

Creating a gifting experience that tells a story on its own, without aesthetically relating back to something specific, can be challenging. My advice is to take the challenge! I think creating lasting and strong connections to the people in your life is always worth the effort. This category of gift recipients likes items to match or coordinate, so if you don't have an existing item to relate a new item to, your new item or items have to be their own complete story.

I love to decorate for holidays and seasons and celebrate the time of year or special occasions that are happening around us. One year on Valentine's Day, I woke up and got the kids dressed for school as usual. When we went downstairs, we found that my husband had decorated the kitchen table with a Valentine's Day tablecloth, plates, and decorations. It was amazing: he had created a gifting experience that celebrated my love for decorating for the holidays, and he had made the kitchen feel perfectly adorned with items that all related! Luckily for him, the items he selected didn't have to match or coordinate with anything existing because I had never decorated our table for Valentine's Day before. It was a very memorable gifting occasion.

The perfectionist category offers a lot of reward for the effort put in. If you have a personality that tends to focus on details already, this category won't be much of a challenge. But if you are someone who can't relate to a particular need for things to be a certain way, this can be a more challenging personality to find a gift for. With all the categories, it is important to understand yourself as well as the recipient.

It's also important to identify which areas of designing a gifting experience may be more challenging to you. If you are finding a gift for someone in the perfectionist category and decision making is something you struggle with, try to come up with a coping mechanism to help get you to the finish line. For instance, if you are great at all aspects of the gifting process except picking which item to get, then bring someone along who can help you with that final step. Don't let one part of the process make you feel unsuccessful overall.

The Collector

The collector is someone who gets excited by groups or sets of items that share similar traits, trends, or brands. This person enjoys receiving things that further the groups of items in his or her life. A collection could be anything from a traditional collection of rare stamps and coins to something nontraditional, like a love for red kitchen accessories.

This category does not just include people who have a traditional collection. In the context of gifting, the collector is a person who appreciates the way things go together in sets. You may have people in your life who are indeed collectors even though they do not have traditional collections.

A favorite example of this personality is my grandmother. I remember the year my mom gave my grandmother a set of dishes that had chickens on them. My grandmother loved the dishes, and the gift was a huge success. My grandmother lives on a farm, and the dishes went perfectly with the feel of her farmhouse. After that, everyone in the family began giving her fun kitchen and home accents that featured chickens. This is not a traditional collection, but because we all began to see these items as related, we approached gifting for her as if we were building on a collection. She loves her chicken-accented kitchen and home.

The way to approach the gifting experience for someone in this category is to really understand what it is about the collection that the person loves. Then choose something that will emotionally connect back to you so that you do not get lost in a sea of similarly detailed items. If someone's collection is extensive, you want to make sure that the piece you give will stand out in some way as unique to your relationship rather than trying to get a unique item in the collection (which may not always be available or affordable).

The collector may also simply enjoy receiving items from one specific category. You might know someone who loves a specific fashion brand or clothing designer or someone who enjoys playing golf and loves new accessories to enhance his game. Often people in this category have specific hobbies and interests that are well known and are a long-standing part of their lives.

Within this category, whether the collection in question is traditional or nontraditional, certain details are important to the recipient. These features include details that relate the items to one another based on, for instance, a physical or functional attribute. When selecting gifts that will be added to a collection of some kind, you want to make sure that you are aware of what the person already has so you don't end up purchasing something that is a duplicate or redundant.

If you are selecting for a person in this category during a time when others are doing the same, it may be helpful to communicate with everyone to make sure your gift selections are known. You could coordinate with other friends or family members to make sure that your gift (as well as the gifts of others) will all collectively go together and make a larger impact on the collection you are adding to.

One year my sister and her husband were moving into a new condo right around her birthday. They had been living in a very small apartment prior, and she was so excited to have a second bedroom to set up as an office. For her birthday I coordinated with the family to give her a collection of new office accessories and picture frames that would make her new space look and feel amazing. Each piece of the set represented everyone in the family, but everything went together as a great collection of beautiful things and made her new office space feel perfect.

When you are choosing a gift for someone who has an existing collection, creativity in both your approach and your presentation will add the personal touch that will make your gift stand out as a connection between the two of you. My dad has a collection of woodworking clamps that take up a small room, but no matter how many clamps he already has in his shop, he loves and appreciates unique additions to his collection. It's a fun challenge to search for different clamps he could use for his woodworking projects. One year I wrapped up a box with some unique clamps inside and then used large clamps, which he always claims to need more of, on the outside of the package in place of ribbon. He was thrilled to have more clamps, and the packaging made the gift memorable and fun to give and receive.

The things that people collect have strong ties to their personalities and interests. Giving gifts that further the traditional and nontraditional collections these individuals love celebrates their unique attributes, and this is an amazing way to build connections with the people around you.

The Undecided

Undecided personalities can't make up their minds about what they want, even when picking things out for themselves. They may not care about specific details relating items together, or they may not be confident in what they like. Decision making can be difficult for this particular personality, and their lives tend to be surrounded with an eclectic array that may or may not coordinate in style, color, or features. People in this category don't follow an analytical path for selecting possessions.

People in this category are usually thrilled when others select items for them because it means that they don't have to. Because these people don't offer many clues, you as the gifter have to compensate. Undecided people can also lack focus, and having few particulars can make it seem like everything is an option. When you have too many choices, it can be overwhelming to figure out how to narrow your search and pinpoint your direction.

With most personalities you begin the gifting process by identifying at least one broad category from which to work. With this category, however, you may also need to identify a secondary influence to guide you down a successful path. The occasion or holiday can become the theme or starting point for creating the broad gifting category to work from.

Gifts that you have enjoyed receiving for similar occasions may help guide you to a great gifting experience for the undecided personality. You can draw on your own experiences to help direct you. For example, if you are celebrating someone's wedding and you are already married, you can think back to the gifts you loved receiving at your wedding.

Typically people who fall into this category are not perfectionists. Because they are not as rigid about all of the items in their lives coordinating aesthetically, there is more room for the things around them to be eclectic. With this in mind, I think of this category as being very accepting of quirky items that may simply speak to you as the gifter or remind you of your friend or family member in the moment and without a great deal of planning.

Doing a lot of preplanning when approaching a gifting occasion for the undecided person in your life may not be of much use. Oftentimes the most successful gifts for this group are found when you are simply out shopping for something that feels right. Being spontaneous and open to finding the right gift will help create a gifting experience that isn't overanalyzed. You may not need to know anything more than the name of a store the person likes in order to begin your quest. Shopping "in the moment" can be very successful for this particular personality.

Undecided people tend to become more undecided when forced to determine whether something meets their requirements because they don't know what their requirements are. Analysis is not part of their decision-making process; for them, decision making is a more spontaneous and emotional process that happens when something feels right. Because their approach is nonanalytical, your approach to finding a gift for them should reflect that same sentiment. Now is the perfect time to shop: find a store that you know has a variety of items that the person might gravitate toward, and let your intuition be your guide.

My sister loves it when someone else decides what she wants and what she should have. I was out shopping one day and came across a very distinct pheasant gravy boat. It was unique, and I instantly knew she would love it. The only connection between the item and her was that she enjoys hosting a large Thanksgiving feast every year: the item didn't specifically match anything she already had, and it wasn't designed to coordinate with her dishes or her kitchen. Yet she loved that gravy boat, and it is one of my favorites among the things I have given her. Every year she gets it out and talks to it as she is filling it with delicious gravy, as though it is part of the family. Her joy for that gift came from its unexpected nature. She hadn't imagined that she needed or wanted it, and yet now she can't live without it.

For me this is the easiest personality to find a gift for, but that is not the case for everyone. I enjoy finding gifts for this personality for two reasons: I like making decisions, and I enjoy going out and shopping for things that make me think of the undecided people in my life. For those who do not like making decisions or do not particularly enjoy the shopping aspect of gift giving, the undecided personality can be the most difficult category. If you do not love to make decisions or shop until a spark of an item strikes you, you need to plan for the time it may take you to find an unplanned gift. Planning for the unplanned will take you in a bit of a circle, but it may help you to feel some element of control in an otherwise free-flowing gifting experience.

Give yourself the time to focus on not overanalyzing the things around you; let yourself relax, and enjoy taking in the things you are considering by paying attention to how the things you see make you feel. Your intuition can be your best guide.

It's fairly easy to relax your analytical side when you are thinking about smaller or less expensive items for people in your life. With this category the more difficult aspect is selecting a more significant piece, something that the person is going to have for a very long time. I was lucky that my sister loved the pheasant gravy boat as much as she did. However, my brother-in-law has many times been faced with purchasing larger or more expensive gifts that he really wanted to make sure she would love. Because those with this personality don't really have a focus or direction for the things they want in life, investing in larger pieces without specific details to reference can be stressful.

In my experience, people with this personality love having their loved ones select an item for them, whether it's a small sauceboat or something larger and more significant. Even though a larger purchase in this category may cause the you to worry, the same principles apply no matter the price point. Anyone who falls into the undecided category does not take an analytical approach to selecting items. Undecided personalities are happy to let things that feel right be a part of their world, no matter what the details or style may be.

When an occasion arises, however significant, and you find yourself looking for a gift for someone with an undecided personality, let yourself shop and find something that feels right without using the analytics and preplanning required for some of the other personalities. This category of gifting is focused on what speaks to you about the person you are giving to. There is always a process to find a gift, and with this personality the story of how you found what you give can be as engaging as the gift itself. Let the full experience, from beginning to end, be the perfect gifting experience for those undecided loved ones in your life.

The Independent

Independent people seem to never need or want anything because if they see something and want it, they will buy it for themselves. They leave little room for anyone to give them anything because the second they say they like something, they have already ordered it online. With this category, attentiveness is not enough to identify the perfect gift since the items they tell you about are most likely already being shipped to their door.

With this personality, their desires seem to be instantaneously met with acquisition, so you have to avoid getting stuck in the middle and simply forge your own path. If you try to outshop them by obtaining something before they can, you may find that the stress leaves you feeling unsuccessful. The impatience of the independent personality can frustrate even the fastest gifter.

Surprise spoilers are a common way to know if you are looking for a gift for a person with a strong, independent personality. You may find that in order to keep such personalities from indulging their impulsive side, you have to drop hints or even tell them ahead of time what you are giving them to avoid duplication. This certainly can be frustrating, not to mention an unexciting way to experience the joy of gifting someone you love and care about.

However, the perception that people in this category purchase everything they want may not be entirely accurate: that may seem to be the case because they purchase the bigger or more obvious things in categories they are interested in. My dad is a skilled woodworker, and has a large woodshop that is seemingly full of all the tools you could imagine he would need and want. Once when I was shopping with him at his favorite woodworking store for a project he was going to do for me, he commented about wanting small endcap items that we passed by as though he didn't have them or needed new ones. I was surprised that there was anything left in the store that he didn't have at home. What I came to know is that because he bought himself the large things he needed for the furniture he made, he didn't buy himself the little accessories because they weren't as necessary at any one particular time.

It turned out that he held back on some of the smaller items to justify the larger purchases. As you can imagine, this opened the door for great gifting ideas for tools, though on a different scale than I would have originally thought. Now instead of searching for one tool to add to his shop, I look for small and interesting accessories that can go with the more obvious things he surely has already.

Another approach is to anticipate something the person will likely buy for himself or herself and then upgrade what he or she would have purchased to make sure your thoughtfulness enhances the gifting experience. My husband wanted to purchase concert tickets for his dad, knowing that his dad would likely want to purchase them for himself. To make sure that the gift didn't lose the special element of surprise, my husband bought much nicer seats than his dad would have. His dad appreciated the upgrade very much because the experience at the concert was so much nicer than what he would have arranged on his own.

The independent personality can present an exciting challenge for someone up for a bit more creative thinking than the other categories require. You have to go outside the bubble. Mixing and matching items to create a customized group of gifts for people with this personality is a great way to create something that is not likely to be similar to something they would have purchased on their own. If most mainstream or obvious items have been secured already, putting together smaller items that may have been overlooked can add up to the same exciting gifting experience as one larger gift.

To be successful in putting together a group of smaller gifts, you want the items to relate, through either the way they will be used or their coordinating aesthetic features. It is unlikely that the person you are giving to would put together the same package of customized items, which makes this a useful way to approach the gifting process for an independent person.

A friend of mine bought her first house, and I wanted to give her a housewarming present. This person really didn't leave much for anyone to gift because she knew exactly what she wanted and obtained it before anyone else could. She had told me that she and her husband had a lot of painting to do when they moved in, and she was looking forward to doing the painting herself and making it their own. I decided that as a housewarming gift, I would put together a painting gift bucket. First I bought nice paintbrushes, nicer brushes than she probably would have bought since they had so many things to purchase for the new home. Then I obtained all the accessories needed to paint and put them together in a bucket from the hardware store with a card made out of paint swatches. It was super fun and a great way to put together a gift that she wouldn't have made for herself.

Consumables, things that are eaten or used within a relatively short amount of time, can also be a good way to add to a gift for this personality. Generally, in this category, you may be looking for more than one gift to ensure personalization. Sure, people with this personality tend to take care of purchasing the items they want, but that doesn't mean they indulge themselves. (Also, if you love a consumable, you can never have enough!) So adding a bit of indulgence to gifts for independent people can be a great way to make them feel special in a way they can't do on their own.

My brother-in-law drinks more coffee than anyone I have ever known. Because he drinks a lot of coffee, he buys a lot of coffee for himself. The large bags of beans that are delivered to his house on a regular basis would generally make me rule out buying him coffee as a gift. But instead of eliminating coffee from my list when thinking about a gift for him, I include it. Since he buys so much coffee, the coffee he buys is not very special. Thus I look for small bags of uniquely roasted beans that are completely different from what he normally consumes in high volumes. He loves receiving those small special bags of coffee, not because he doesn't have enough coffee, but because he never takes the time to search out specialty roasts for himself.

You may also find that the independent nature of this personality exists only within a select group of categories. It could be that your friend or family member is extremely independent about buying clothes they want but do not buy movies or books that they are interested in. In this case finding the right gift may be about identifying the category the person overlooks. You can be successful in purchasing for any personality type if you are open to understanding what excites and motivates the people in your life.

Of course, not everyone will fit perfectly into one of the eight categories outlined in this book. In fact most people are a combination of several. Understanding the unique combinations that make up the people in your life helps bring variety and personalization to the gifting experience.

Some people exhibit different gifting personalities depending on what category of gift you are looking at. My husband, for instance, doesn't fit into the new hotness category for most gifts—unless you are talking about coffee. If there is a gift related to his beloved coffee, he wants the latest and greatest. Understanding that he only exhibits this personality for one specific category reminds me to use that mind-set only when I am giving him coffee.

The next chapter, about gifting occasions, can help you determine which gifting personality to focus on depending on the occasion. The occasion itself often helps to narrow the type of gift you are looking for, and from there you can identify which gifting personality is most appropriate.

Chapter 3
Why Are You Giving?

Any occasion for gifting allows us insight into the roots of our desire to connect with the people in our lives. When you understand the occasion you are gifting for, you understand the next step—building a connection through the gifts you give.

Taking a moment to reflect upon the meaning behind the occasions you celebrate gives you another important piece in assembling the gifting experience. If you know that you are celebrating someone's birthday through a gift, then focusing on the joy you feel for that person individually will help to focus your gifting experience. Some occasions for gifting are not as singularly focused. Occasions that are celebrated by a group, a family, or a couple, change the way you should approach gifting.

Gifting is often linked closely to celebration. A celebration can be a large number of people gathering for the holidays or a small number of people celebrating the wedding of a close friend. Millions of people all over the world might be celebrating simultaneously, or two people may be celebrating their wedding anniversary alone. Understanding why you are giving a gift is an important component in designing the perfect gifting experience. If you don't know why you are giving a gift, you are going to have a hard time figuring out how to give something meaningful.

The best gifts come from a place of caring and should not be thought of as obligatory. That might seem idealistic, as gifts are often an important component in cultural celebrations and rituals and can have a strong tie to etiquette and long-standing social protocol. But the gifting element of any celebration should always enhance the celebration's meaning and significance by creating closer emotional connections to the ones with whom you are celebrating.

When you receive a wedding invitation in the mail, you are being invited to the couple's celebration of their future life together. The gift you bring to them should thus be an expression of your joy and happiness for their celebration. You are showing through the manifestation of your expressive self that you are happy for them in their new life as a couple, and you want them to remember your joy for their celebration through a gift they will have and share in their married life.

When my husband and I got married, a good family friend of mine gave us an engraved chip and dip bowl as a wedding present. It was beautiful, and it reminded me of the Super Bowl parties that this family friend used to host when I was a kid. The gift was a wonderful connector, and, owning it, I have felt inspired to host my own Super Bowl parties.

Exploring the deeper meaning behind the occasions you celebrate helps you to uphold the joyful memories of wonderful occasions together. A gift carries with it the connections to your friends and family and the joyful feelings you have when you celebrate with the people closest to you.

The gifts exchanged between two significant others to celebrate an anniversary are a way to link the past, present, and future of the relationship. When you exchange such gifts, you are celebrating a day that is in the past while enjoying the present moment together and looking forward to the joy you feel for the future. Taking this into consideration, you would want to give something that holds components of each of these elements. You want an anniversary gift to be something that has connections to the past but also looks joyfully to the future.

You could put together a frame or photo book with pictures from the past of you and your significant other. You might even include photos of your ancestors to create a link between your heritage and the present day. Whatever you choose, you should leave room for future pictures and memories. Along with this gesture, you could give the gift of a new camera to help capture those future moments. If the person in your life already has a camera and isn't in the market for a new one, you could go the less traditional and less expensive route and give a vintage-inspired instant camera. An anniversary celebrates a time when you were younger and perhaps more spontaneous, and pictures are a great way to capture and remember those times together.

There are three types of occasions on which you express yourself through gifting: the main two are special occasions and spontaneous events that come up through life experiences. The third is no occasion at all: sometimes we give gifts just because we care for and love the people in our lives.

Special Occasions

First, and most common, are special occasions. Some occasions on which you might give gifts to your friends and family include birthdays, anniversaries, graduations, weddings, births, holidays, and retirements. You might even bring hostess gifts to parties throughout the year. Special-occasion gifts are given to celebrate or honor a specific event, either in the calendar year or in someone's life.

Because there are so many special occasions each year, you may find these instances to be fraught with expectations that create stress and pressure around otherwise happy, joyful celebrations. The number of gifting occasions throughout the year can be intimidating. Your goal should be to get away from these negative emotions and turn the experience of gifting into something positive and fun. Gifting should be part of the joy of celebrating with the people in your life and show appreciation for the people around you.

You want to be open and expressive in the special occasions you celebrate. If you fully celebrate your loved ones and express your joy for the special moments in life, you will find reward within yourself. Embracing the special moments in life brings a renewed sense of appreciation for the special occasions of the past and a hopeful look forward to special occasions in the future.

The reason for the celebration should be the foundation of your gifting approach for any special occasion. Celebrating someone's birthday, for example, is always a link back to the past since the occasion is centered on that person's birth. I love when birthday cards and birthday surprises are focused on baby pictures and funny birthday memories. I used to ask my mom for a cheesecake as my birthday cake when I was little, so when my husband gets me a cheesecake just like the ones I loved when I was little, it's a sweet birthday gesture.

Spontaneous Occasions

The second reason we give gifts is spontaneity. Examples of spontaneous gifting are thank-you gifts, get-well gifts, gifts to encourage or to celebrate an accomplishment, and even "I'm sorry" gifts. Spontaneous gifts are different because they aren't restricted by the same expectations as special-occasion gifts regarding what they should be or how they should be presented. They are more specific to the moment. You may go your entire life without ever having to give someone an "I'm sorry" gift, or you may have to give many.

My husband put his wedding band in the pocket of a pair of shorts he was wearing while working on a project. He completely forgot about the ring and later threw the shorts in the laundry. I found the wedding ring, thankfully, but I was not thrilled that he had been so forgetful. As an "I'm sorry" gesture, he brought home a bouquet of flowers that looked just like our wedding flowers and got a lovely dessert for after dinner. Then he put on the song we'd danced to at our reception and asked me to dance with him in our kitchen. It was very thoughtful, and through his gift he both reminded me how much he loved our wedding day and expressed how sorry he was to have been careless with his wedding ring. This gift turned the experience into a happy memory that we still laugh about today.

When it comes to spontaneous experiences in your life when you feel a gift would be appreciated, you should not rely on a repetitive meaning for a specific occasion to guide you to the emotions you want to convey. Instead use empathy for the recipient's situation to support him or her with a gift that mirrors the emotions of the occasion.

The most important thing to keep in mind when selecting a spontaneous gift is why you are giving the gift. Knowing why will guide you to the emotions you want to express through the gift. For instance, if you are giving a gift to thank someone, you should take time to consider how that person's actions made you feel. Your gift should help express your appreciation for the emotions you felt.

I love thank-you gifts because of their very nature: someone has touched your life in some way, and you feel joy in showing him or her appreciation. I was out to dinner one evening and happened to see my daughter's teacher out at the same restaurant. Her teacher was amazing, and the appreciation I felt for his dedication was something I wanted to put into a tangible gift at the end of the school year. I remember that when I saw him out at dinner, I almost felt as though I had seen a celebrity. At the end of the year, I gave him a gift card to the restaurant we had seen him at, and I told him the story of how he was our celebrity. My daughter made him a card, and we put all the thought we could into giving him a gift that made him feel special.

A gift should add joy to any occasion. On a spontaneous occasion, you are either adding more joy to an already positive situation or adding joy to an otherwise negative situation. Whether you are showing appreciation or trying to lift a person up during a difficult time, your reflection of the specific occasion is the key to expressing yourself in a meaningful way.

Spontaneous gifts are an important way to connect with the people around you in the moment. Unlike with gifts that are given at predictable times of the year, you may not have a lot of time to plan out what you wish to give. I like to use gifts that are consumable and will be acquired and experienced for a finite and sometimes short period of time when I am giving a spontaneous gift. The challenge with consumable gifts is personalizing them to the occasion.

A bottle of wine or a bouquet of flowers will not be experienced physically forever. Spontaneous gifting occasions pair nicely with consumable gifts because they can mirror the amount of time the spontaneous occasion itself lasts. A bottle of wine brought as a hostess gift is lovely because it can be enjoyed for the time that you are at the party. It mirrors the positive sentiments of the occasion.

Some spontaneous occasions and gifts are experienced for a longer period of time. A locket to remember a loved one who has passed away, for example, will be enjoyed for a very long time. Whether you are planning to celebrate a moment of accomplishment or honor a lifetime, both you and the recipient should feel a connection to the occasion. Unlike gifts given for a recurring event, which focus more on the individual receiving the gift, spontaneous gifts often have a greater focus on the reason for gifting. With spontaneous gifting you should use the occasion as your foundation for planning a meaningful gift.

No Occasion

The third, and most often overlooked, reason we give gifts is for no reason at all. This is my personal favorite type of gifting, even if it is the least common. With the spirit of being expressive and joyful in mind, it is always great to give something to someone just because you thought of him or her. You might be out and see something that reminds you of a person in your life, or you may think of something special that you would like to do for someone. Don't ever hold back if you feel like showing someone how you feel through a gift. The more joy we give to others, the happier we make ourselves. Smiles and laughter tied up in a package can be the best way to wrap the earth with joy and delight.

I am always trying to figure out ways to manifest the concept of living in the moment. Gifting allows me to experience more presently the joy I feel and the appreciation I have for the people around me. When I think of someone I love or see something that reminds me of a friend or family member, I try to do something special or give something special to that person. By acting on my joyful thoughts, I am able to build and expand upon relationships and capture joyful moments before they slip away.

Chapter 4
What Are You Giving?

We are exploring the who, why, and what of gifting. So far we have seen that the who and the why provide thought-provoking inspiration to help us gather gifting ideas. We can build successful gifting experiences from the ground up by understanding the recipient's personality and our own reason for giving. With this solid foundation to work from, we move into the object of our attention—the what.

A gift not only connects the recipient to an object or experience; it also connects the recipient to you, the gifter. You want the gifts you give to create an emotional connection between yourself and the people in your life. Giving a gift is not fulfilling an obligation. You are creating an emotional imprint on the people you care about so that joy is expressed out into the world and reflected back on you. If the gifts you give leave no impression, then you have missed an opportunity to create a deeper connection with the people in your life.

By being open and expressive with gifting, you are opening up a part of yourself to the people around you. The object itself is not the gift; the gift is the physical manifestation of your expressive self. Through the experience of giving, you can open your own life and the lives of others to the joy you feel and the happiness the people around you bring. Giving a gift can change someone's life, and it can change yours as well.

Through the manifestation of your joy and happiness, you can enlighten others' senses and form a closer emotional connection. If you feel joyful about what you are giving to someone and the experience of giving helps you develop a closer connection to that person, then you have a gift!

While there is never a bad time to give a gift to express your feelings for a person, celebrations in your life are the perfect time to enjoy a break from your everyday routine. You look forward to those special times every year when you can celebrate with your friends and family and leave behind the necessary selfishness that dominates the majority of your days. Allowing yourself to be immersed in the joy of designing the perfect gifting experience for someone you love and care about is a true celebration of life and something you should experience as often as possible.

Knowing how your gift, whether physical or experiential, will be received is an important component to understanding what you are giving as a gift. Gifts come in all shapes and sizes. Some gifts are easily wrapped up and tied with a pretty bow while others are unwrapped through life adventures. Since gifts are experienced through our senses, a recipient can experience a gift by seeing, feeling, hearing, smelling, or tasting. Some gifts may be multifaceted or experienced through a combination of senses. Creating a gifting experience that is rich in sensory exploration can create a memorable experience for the person in your life.

Our minds retain memories through sensory information, so being cognizant of the senses involved in experiencing a gift will help you to find something that will enrich the recipient's memories of that experience. Often, we relive nostalgic experiences from childhood through familiar smells, colors, or tastes. All of the senses can hold strong ties to memories from our past. A gift such as a bouquet of flowers, a box of chocolates, a card made using a favorite photo, or any item or experience that represents the recipient's style and personality will be incredibly rich in sensory involvement. Such an experience becomes memorable because it can potentially involve all five senses.

I have a good friend who has always wanted to learn to cook, so for her birthday one year, I planned a cooking class that we could attend along with a few other friends of ours. We had a great time being together and engaged in an activity that can be remembered by all the senses it involved. Another idea is to plan a surprise experience to make wine together with your significant other. Taking home a bottle or two of your own creation will have a big impact on all of the senses and create a lasting memory. This is definitely on my list of future gifting ideas for my husband.

When you give someone a gift that he or she absolutely loves, that person immediately wants to experience the gift through the senses it was designed to invigorate. Someone might want to try on new clothes right away or immediately put on a new piece of jewelry. Or a recipient might taste delicious chocolates or smell beautiful flowers right as they are delivered. When a gift hits the mark, the senses will instantly be involved in the experience.

A gift is the object of attention when it is received and the way you communicate your feelings. The thinking and planning stages of the gifting experience can be vague; so early in the process, you may not need the exact answer to feel successful. And while thinking and planning are very necessary, this chapter is about moving beyond those steps and making the choice to give a gift, the object of creating successful gifting experiences. You often need to push yourself when it comes to this final step of decision making and procurement. As you proceed through the process of designing a gifting experience, let this chapter ground you and help you to materialize the philosophical foundation set down in the previous chapters.

Chapter 5
Your Personal Touches

Making sure you are a part of the gifts you give is the final component to designing the perfect gifting experience. When you are giving a gift, you are giving a part of yourself through your emotional expression. Thus it is always important to incorporate your own personal touches into the gifts you give.

I like to think of personal touches as the bow on the presentation of your gift. Your personality doesn't have to be the predominant feature of the gifts you give, but there should be a component of yourself that connects you to the gift.

A good family friend of mine once gave me a beautiful silver cake knife and server for a wedding shower gift. She told me that for her wedding she had been given a similar set and had loved using it for special occasions thereafter. She said the gift had become very special over the years and that it always made her think fondly of the person who had given it to her. That set ended up being one of my favorite wedding gifts because I could feel the emotional connection my friend had with the gift. I think about her every time I get out our cake knife and server, and we use it for all family celebrations. It is one of the most memorable wedding gifts that we received because of the personal connection she gave to us through her gift.

Special touches are appropriate in all aspects of the gifting experience. You can make a gift personal through a handwritten card, special packaging, or even the verbal presentation of your gift. Extra details about the gift you have selected or a story about why the item is special or unique can subtly transform the gifting experience and affirm the emotional connection between you and the person you are giving to.

Your personal involvement in the gifting experience is a form of self-expression and your means of connecting to the people in your life. Taking the time to do the extra things that make a gift unique to both you and the person you are giving to will strengthen the relationships you have. Gifts come in all shapes, sizes, and price points, but no matter how big or small a gift is, the personalization—how you wrap it, present it, or send it—should not be overlooked.

Cards, wrapping paper, boxes, ribbons, and bows—all of these things can be tailored to represent both you and the person you are giving to. You may tell yourself you don't have time or that you are not creative enough to wrap presents in a unique way, but if you consider the presentation of your gift as part of the gift itself, you will see how important it is to make time for the gift as a whole.

I talk about gifts as being more than just gifts; they are experiences between two or more people. Gifts are touched, seen, heard, smelled, and tasted. There is excitement and anticipation when your senses are engaged in the experience of unwrapping the layers of something someone has given to you. Receiving a thoughtful gift causes someone to feel special, and the feeling of opening a unique gift created just for you is powerful and positive. In both giving and receiving, we want to feel the power behind the kind gesture of care and acknowledgment.

One of the hardest types of gifting is finding something for a person you do not know well. Sometimes a gifting occasion is a matter of social protocol, not celebration. I was invited to the wedding of a cousin I hadn't seen in many years. I wanted to send a thoughtful gift, but I didn't know the couple at all. I went to their registry to search for an item that I felt connected to and saw that they were registered for a Chemex pour-over coffee maker. It was great—I had given my husband the exact same one many years ago, and he and I both loved making coffee in it! Because I was able to select something personal, I was able to write a thoughtful note about the gift. Using my own personal touches, I was able to feel connected to their celebration through my gift, despite our lack of familiarity.

Through this book, you have explored the connections between you and the people you are giving to, the occasions you are giving for, and the gifts themselves, and through this you have learned the tools that will help you at all points of the gifting experience. Personal touches are the final piece of designing any gifting experience, as you must put yourself into every gift you give.

Chapter 6
The Gift of Money

A gift should be a form of emotional connection between you and the person you care about. If the gifts you give leave no impression on you or the recipient, then you have lost an opportunity to create a deeper connection with that person in your life. Money can be a thoughtful and expressive gift if it is a joyful expression of your happiness for the occasion.

You should always consider whether money is appropriate for the occasion. For example, the gift of money would generally not be appropriate if given on a relationship-centered occasion between a spouse and significant other. A good rule of thumb is to only give money as a gift for occasions that are centered on life transitions. Money is thoughtful to a recipient who is going off to college, getting married, moving into his or her first house, or bringing a new baby home from the hospital. These occasions are great examples of life transitions. Extra money during life transitions is always helpful and therefore can be a good gift to consider for these events. However, the money should be given in a way that still conveys your thoughtfulness. It should also be presented to create a lasting memory and connection with the person you are giving to.

The gift of money can lose its meaning if the right experience isn't designed around it. You must not let money be a fallback simply because nothing else comes to mind. If money is being used because it's "easy," then you are removing the emotional involvement and thought that should be included with your gift.

When we experience major transitions in life, stress regarding new or added expenses can cloud our joy. A gift of money can reduce the stress individuals or couples feel when they are going through a life transition. Money can help to enhance the joy you want your friends and family to feel in their new life adventures.

If you are considering giving the gift of money to someone in your life, you should make sure that your joy for the special occasion is conveyed in the gifting experience. This means making the gift personal to you and the recipient. This can be as simple as including a nice note in the card, offering a suggestion for how the money can be used, or including a complementary item that helps to fully complete the gifting experience.

Example 1: Congratulations on your beautiful new baby girl! Here is a little something to help fill up her piggy bank.

You could include a gift of a piggy bank with the new baby's name painted on the side, along with a check or cash gift inside the card.

Example 2: Congratulations on buying your first house! The pictures of your new backyard are amazing. Here is a little something to help jump-start your gardening tool collection.

You could include a gift of gardening gloves for the new homeowners, along with a check or cash gift inside the card.

Example 3: Congratulations on your wedding—we are so happy for you both and excited for your new life together. We hope you have a wonderful honeymoon in the Bahamas. Please use this gift to treat yourselves to breakfast in bed while enjoying a view of the ocean!

You could include a printed-out room-service menu from the hotel that the couple will be staying at or use the menu as a jumping-off point for a homemade card.

In these examples each gift is meaningful and personal and clearly designed to express joy and develop a deeper connection between giver and recipient.

When my husband and I bought our first house, one of our relatives sent us a housewarming card with a personal note that read, "We noticed in the pictures of your kitchen that you were missing a refrigerator. Please use this gift to buy one!" It was so thoughtful and unexpected. The person couldn't pick out a refrigerator for us, but the fact that he included such a personal note made us feel as though he did. Thus a joyful connection was made through a gift of money. And even though that check went into an account that paid for many new things, it always felt as though he had given us a gift of a refrigerator. Even many years later, I often think of how unexpected and exciting it was to receive such a nice gift.

Here are a few more examples of creative ways to present the gift of money to your friends and family.

Example 1: If you knew that a close family member was trying to save for a new house, you could construct a house out of paper money, making the roof removable, and fill the inside with the recipient's favorite candy. (I actually did this, and it was hilarious! After a month or so, the family member asked if he could take the house apart and use the money. I laughed and said, "Of course—that is what it is for!" I should have included that in the card!)

Example 2: As a gift for a guy, you could purchase a money clip with the recipient's initials engraved on the front and then place a cash gift inside the clip.

Example 3: For a high-school graduate about to face coin-operated laundry at college, you could fill a laundry basket with detergent, a laundry bag embroidered with the recipient's name (or initials) on the front, and a large jar already filled with enough quarters for many months of laundry. You could even make a creative label for the front of the jar to act as a card and encourage the college-bound loved one to remember to do her laundry.

The important rule to remember when giving money is that you should not give cash to avoid having to put in the time and effort required to find a meaningful gift. If you do not express yourself through the gift, you cannot expect the recipient to feel a personal connection to you through the gift. Gifts should be memorable and build deeper and more meaningful connections with the people in your life.

Cash isn't the only way to give the gift of money. Gift cards and online store credits are more popular than ever. Gift cards offer an opportunity to tailor the gift of money so that it is used at a specific place or for a specific item. Millions of people every year set out on a path to give someone something and end up talking themselves into a gift card because they are sure it will be more appreciated than something they might choose.

Like cash, gift cards should not be a replacement for taking the time to think through the best gift. Gifting can be challenging, but that makes it all the more rewarding as a result. A gift card can be great for the person in your life who seeks unique experiences that can't be put in a box or in situations where you can't be present in the gifting experience due to distance or other circumstances. In some situations, sending an object to someone is not possible, and a gift card may be perfect.

The key to turning a plastic card into a memorable gift is finding a unique way to express yourself through it to make sure your personal expression of joy is not lost. You may be able to think of a unique way to present the gift card, or you might select a card to a place that has meaning to you and the person you are giving to. You can also be specific about what you want the person to buy with the gift card to help form an emotional connection between you and the item eventually purchased.

Example 1: One year, for Mother's Day, my sisters and I weren't able to be at home with my mom to celebrate the occasion. Even though we couldn't be with her, we wanted to let her know how much we were thinking about her, so we planned a day of fun experiences using gift cards. I wrote her the following card and sent it along with a gift card for her favorite ice-cream treat, a gift card to her favorite garden store, and a gift card for a hot stone massage:

> We can't be with you today, so we thought we'd plan a few things to let you know how much we're thinking about you on Mother's Day!
>
> You always made sure we ate breakfast in the morning before school, so why not begin your day with a lovely banana split from Dairy Queen?
>
> You always made sure we were not afraid to get our hands dirty, so take a stop at your favorite gardening store to enjoy some new plants for spring.

Now we think it's time for you to relax with a hot stone massage, and don't forget to grab one of your favorite Snickers! Know that we love you and are thinking about you on Mother's Day!

Included with the gift cards was a new pair of gardening gloves and a bag of her favorite Snickers Miniatures. Sending her a gift card to buy an inexpensive item like a banana split might seem unorthodox, but how much she loves to get a banana split from Dairy Queen right when the weather gets warm is something that makes her special, and celebrating what makes someone special creates joyful connections. In this example my sisters and I used personal, sentimental touches in our card to create an experience designed to make sure my mom knew how much we loved and appreciated her.

Example 2: For Father's Day one year, my sisters and I wanted to give my dad the gift of golfing at a great golf course in our area. Since you can't wrap up a round of eighteen, we used a gift card to give my dad the experience. To make sure we didn't lose our own expression of love for him in the gift, I designed a handmade card with pictures and information about the course he would be playing, and we invited his favorite golf buddy to accompany him for the day. We wanted to make sure that my dad made an emotional connection with us through our gift. Including the course information in our card meant he instantly had something tactile to experience, read through, and talk about, and that helped Dad make an instant connection to the experience to come. My sisters and I got to see and participate in the excitement while he was looking ahead and analyzing how his golf game would play out.

Something that is very important to consider when giving someone a gift card is the potential lapse between when the card is given and when the full experience of the gift will take place. When there is a gap between the initial presentation of the gift and the experience of the gift, it is important that you give the person something to physically begin to build excitement and anticipation for the future.

Example 3: A few years ago, my sisters and I wanted to give my mom a new purse for her birthday. We had tried in the past to purchase an actual purse, without any success. We knew that a gift card would be fun, but we wanted it to feel personal. To present my mom with her new purse, I wrote her a poem about the adventure of finding a new purse, and I planned an outing for my sisters and I to go with my mom to shop for one. Along with the poem, we included a gift card for the purchase of the new purse and a basket of fun items you might find in a purse so there would be something tactile to explore and have fun with prior to our outing. We then went along and made a fun day of selecting a purse she loved. Below is the poem.

> A new purse for Jill
> Wouldn't that be a thrill
> Something stylish but subtle
> What a large bill to fill
> This one black, this one brown
> This one tall, this one small
> So many to choose from here at the mall
> Zippers a plenty and pockets galore
> Every which way we turn there seem to be more
> Will this one be right; oh, I'm just not so sure
> We wanted to find one that was just right for you
> So we'll set out again but come much more prepared
> We'll take you along; yes, that will work great
> Too excited to wait we'll head out half past eight
> Let's meet up for breakfast pancakes for all
> We'll need it to make it all day at the mall
> At ten on the dot the sales teams will be ready
> The purses assembled lined up on the shelves
> Oh, this may take Santa or at least one of his elves
> We'll try them all on stare close in the mirror
> Surely one will shine brighter; it will become so much clearer
> We'll leave when we've concurred a new purse for Jill
> A new purse for Jill; oh, this will be a thrill
> Happy Birthday!

My sisters and I were able to express our joy for my mom and celebrate with her on her birthday, but we used a gift card to allow Mom to find the right purse and complete the perfect experience. Celebrating the things that make people unique is fun. As long as I can remember, my mom has been incredibly particular about the purse she carries, so it was fun to celebrate that aspect of her personality. We were able to show her how well we knew her and how much we love her!

If you aren't much of a poet or the idea of creating a custom card makes you want to run for the hills, stick with the idea that thoughtful touches will make your gifts more successful and in turn bring you closer to the people in your life. I have gathered these examples over decades of gifting occasions. I reserve extra creative touches for times when the gifts are more experiential and therefore require more personalized elements to create the meaningful connections I want to have.

With any gift of money, adding a personalized touch is key to making sure the gift doesn't fall short of emotional connectedness. A gift card represents a gift that is going to be purchased or experienced at a later time, so you should include something physical that can be opened at the gifting moment. A physical component to bridge the original gifting moment with the eventual gifting moment is very important in building the immediate connection between you, the gift, and the person you are giving to.

The gift of money is a way to broaden the range of gifts and experiences you are able to offer. Through the gift of money, you have the power to create experiences that otherwise would not fit in a box or under a tree. But with this expansion of capabilities, you want to make sure to retain the purpose and meaning of the gifting experience: to give of yourself and create personal and joyful experiences and lasting connections.

Conclusion

Throughout my life I have been influenced by the gifts I have received as well as the gifts I have given. I value feeling loved and emotionally connected to friends and family. Giving gifts is the best way I have found to live presently and joyfully. I embrace formal gifting occasions while also thoroughly enjoy the spontaneity of finding something unique that simply makes me think of someone in my life. Through the gifts I give, I give a part of myself. It is through this expression that I emotionally connect to the people in my life and feel more connected to myself.

I use the gifting philosophies and methods from this book to help guide my approach to gifting. I understand who am I giving to, why am I giving, what I am giving, how my gift will be received, and what personal touches are important to ensure that my emotions are felt through my gift. This creates a foundation for narrowing the categories at the beginning of my gifting search and helps me with decision-making parameters for purchasing my gift. Using these methods, I feel confident that I can design the perfect gifting experience for everyone in my life.

Enjoy yourself when giving to others. Your passion for the people you care about will ultimately be your guide to finding the perfect gift and creating an experience that instills lasting joyful memories and deeper personal connections.

We give gifts to honor and celebrate special occasions, moments, and everyday experiences. We invite warm and joyful moments into our lives by giving a piece of ourselves in the things we wrap up for others. The occasion of gifting can be a wonderful expression of the best aspects of our world. We should embrace every opportunity we find to give more to one another.

I have worked on writing this book for over ten years. A lot of emotional travel was necessary for me to comprehend the deeper meaning behind the message I was searching for. My mind has been open to understanding this topic through personal experience. I am forever grateful for the journey I have taken in discovering how to live more presently through the gifts that I give.

It is with joy that I give this philosophy of gifting to you.

www.ingramcontent.com/pod-product-compliance
Lightning Source LLC
Chambersburg PA
CBHW070204060426
42445CB00032B/1347